"Become a Sonographer"

Foreword

I have been a sonographer for the past eighteen years and was clinical instructor for our facility in cardiac and general ultrasound for five of those. Several times a month our department receives requests asking for job shadows from eager students that want to join the profession. Some of these people have gone on to be exceptional sonographers but the reality is most that apply to the program usually are not accepted.

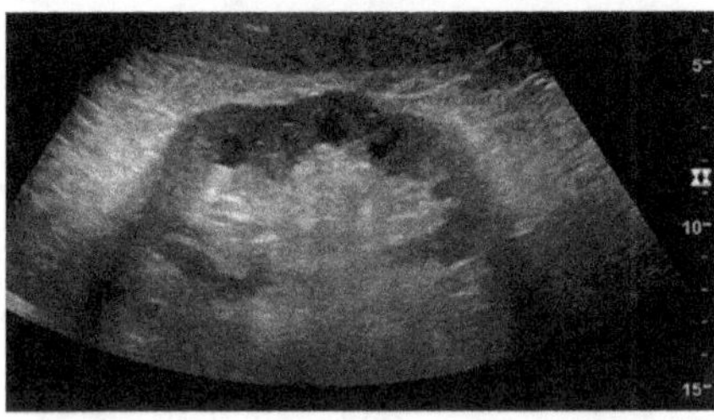

Sonography is a unique learning process, and for that reason the programs are only able to accept a limited number of students at a time. It is common to have ten or fifteen times the number of applicants to available spots and it is important that you set yourself apart. It is also very important that you know what is involved with being a sonographer, the application process and the course work.

The main reason for this guide is that over countless coffee meetings I have listened to numerous people tell me "I want to be an ultrasound technician." I am glad there is so much interest but after a while it is like a song you have heard on the radio over and over.   I will try to help you by providing some information of what a sonographer (that was lesson 1) does, what is involved with the day to day aspects of the job, how to work through the application process, some specific interview tips and what to expect from the training.

Knowing what is involved is very important in deciding if sonography is a good career fit for you. Many people dedicate a significant amount of time and resources to gain entry to a sonography program only to find out that it is not what they initially thought or what they wanted to do. Hopefully, this booklet will aid you in that decision.

I applaud your interest in ultrasound as a profession. It is an incredibly diverse field and evolves very quickly. Hang on and have fun!

Good luck,

Bernard "Buzz" Cox

Part 1 - Why Become a Sonographer?

So, you have an interest in becoming a sonographer. As mentioned previously, I think it is a great profession and can certainly understand your enthusiasm. But how did that interest come about? Do you know someone that works in the profession? Did you read about how the job market for sonographers is very healthy and decided you wanted some job security? Did you see someone getting an ultrasound on a medical program? Did you get scanned yourself? It is important to ask where this motivation came from.

Ultrasound like any career is a decision that should be made with some research and thought. If you want to enter the profession because "scanning babies" seemed cool well trust me, the shine on that finish wears off very quickly for most. This book will go into most of the areas that ultrasound covers and help you decide if it is the right choice because babies are a small fraction of what most sonographers do, It just usually gets the most press.

Potential students often ask, "what are the qualities required to be a good sonographer." That is a good question and much like the profession it is very subjective. Ask yourself if any or all of these describe you!

Properties of a good sonographer.

The interview panel will most likely ask you about these. See the interview questions in appendix A under "self-assessment."

Dedication:

To get in and last in ultrasound you must be dedicated to the process. It is a rigorous application and training course and once you are finished training it requires you to maintain your competence with continuing education and constant learning. Ultrasound technology is evolving continuously (a lot of which I use today was not even thought of 10 years previously!) and with new technology there are always new techniques and protocols to learn. If you are the type of person that thinks once the training is done you can just coast, this is not the case.

Flexibility:

With ultrasound you learn how to scan and recognize normal and abnormal anatomy. Every patient is different, so you must be ready to vary your scanning techniques to achieve diagnostic results.

There is quite a variety of ultrasound machines that are in use today. You may work in a department that uses different types of systems and you really must be able to change your thought process to adapt to the individual nuances of each ultrasound unit. An old and tired analogy used compares ultrasound machines to vehicles. There are brand new $100,000 luxury SUV's and there are $1,000 rusty 3rd hand jalopies. They will both get you to where you are going - probably - but some will do it easier, are less stressful to operate and have more options!

You must be able to adapt to the ever-changing demands of the job itself. Usually you come into work and have a room with scheduled patients. This is great but what happens if the machine fails to boot up? What do you do if a patient does not show up or a patient shows up that is scheduled on a different day that has travelled a great distance? What do you do if your colleague with a full slate of patients calls in sick and they cannot get a hold of people to cancel or do not cancel patients as a rule?

These examples represent a minuscule amount of the possible modifications you will encounter at some point. If you are the type of person that enjoys something being the same way every day, then sonography might not the best career choice.

Humility:

To say sonographers have screwed up and missed stuff in their careers is a profound understatement. It is unfortunately the nature of the profession that mistakes happen, but you must be ready to learn from them. Most sonographers have made some kick butt catches scanning but usually cannot reiterate any of them apart from vague details. They will be able to tell you exactly (down to probably the thought process) when they missed a heart defect almost ten years ago. The sooner you accept that learning hard lessons is the reality the sooner you will be on your way to becoming a good and competent sonographer.

Empathy:

This particular property is debatable. Some people say that they do not give a rip about the patient, their situation and they insist that it does not affect how they scan this person. Overall, many people find this hard to believe and take a different view. One of my colleagues explained it well when she said this patient is *someone's* mom, dad or child so why should we treat them any different than my own.

Most in our profession have some degree of empathy either inherent or earned. It might stem from the fact that we are in close proximity to a patient for an extended period.

Attention to Detail:

For sonographers, it is critical to be attentive to all the little details for a successful scan. You must listen to the patient's signs and symptoms, interpret what you are seeing on the screen correctly and manipulate a very complicated machine to record diagnostic information.

This might sound routine but remember that abnormalities or malignancies can be subtle so looking for these changes in the "snowstorm" of ultrasound is quite important.

For each exam sonographers follow a flowchart called a protocol. This must be adhered to so that each organ of interest is investigated and required images are recorded for the doctor to make the correct diagnosis.

Being a little anal retentive and obsessive compulsive does not hurt either! We just call it "attention to detail!"

Interpersonal Skills:

This is a little different than empathy but is applicable at the same time. People that are having an ultrasound are there to figure out if something is wrong. They are apprehensive or just plain scared and you must deal with them for the length of the examination. This can be 15 to 45 minutes or more so you must interact with them in such a way that you are able to record a history and then perform the scan without being distracted.

This can sound easy but throw in a hundred reasons from the person being in excruciating pain, cultural differences/language or they just do not like you. Most scans go well but some you will be in for a wild ride if you do not know how to handle these situations.

Physical Stamina

This trait is very important and one that you will have limited control over. It may appear that sonographers squirt jelly on the patient and then move the transducer around to get some pictures. I heard an expression once that was very applicable to getting diagnostic images in ultrasound: "the closer the flashlight is to the target, the brighter the beam."

Keeping this analogy in mind, sonographers push, pull and do what it takes to apply pressure in some very awkward positions that would make an occupational therapist or kinesiologist cringe! We must hold these positions sometimes for extended periods of time to record images that are diagnostic quality.

See the section on repetitive strain injuries to give you some strategies to reduce the frequency and severity of them, but understand that continuing to scan works similar to erosion where the wind and water eventually will wear the land down.

One thing you cannot control is how your body is built. Long or short arms are things are just he cards you will have to play, and you must develop unique scanning strategies that will work for you. A good training program with experienced clinical instructors will guide you and adapt to the challenges you and your body will face when scanning patients of all sizes.

Tech Savvy:

You do not have to be a "geek" to be a good sonographer, but it does not hurt! Ultrasound machines are very complicated computers so understanding how to operate, maintain and troubleshoot them will be a not so insignificant part of your training and eventual role.

All imaging is done digitally now so there will be special computers called PACS (Picture Archiving and Communication Systems) that allow you to view your images and possibly RIS (Radiology Information System) that you will have to work with when reporting your cases.

Do not worry if you are not brilliant in this area as you will learn all of this in school. Just remember if this is an area that is not your strong point you may have to spend more time and effort working on this during your training and eventual career.

These are some of the properties that are important to succeeding as a sonographer. People might disagree with some of these or have more to add and that is great – feedback is always graciously accepted!

Part II - The Application Process

Applying:

Training Programs:

When investigating an ultrasound training program, you came across one that is just down the street. Well that is most convenient! You should check a few things out before you dedicate yourself and your cash to "Buzz School of Ultrasound."

In the United States there are numerous colleges and universities that offer a diverse listing of programs. They can be one-year specialty training, two-year associate degree or four-year degree programs. A good thing to verify is that they are accredited by the Commission on Accreditation of Allied Health Education Programs (CAAHEP - https://www.caahep.org/). This will ensure that the training adheres to minimum standards that are required to perform the actual job!

A good thing to verify is that after you complete your training you will be eligible to write certification exams such as the American Registry of Diagnostic Medical Sonographers (ARDMS). Most employers and states are requiring certification before they will even consider you for a position.

In Canada, all formal sonography training programs are accredited Accreditation Canada and after the training are eligible to write the ARDMS exams. The licensing body in Canada is called Sonography Canada (SC) and they administer their own set of examinations several times a year.

SC takes a different type of philosophy with their process as there is a competency component. This means in addition theoretical examinations there is a minimum number of exams (competencies) that must be *observed* before the individual is eligible for an ultrasound credential. Most employers in Canada are asking for the Canadian credential as it ensures that a minimum standard has been met from both didactic and scanning perspectives. This usually verifies that the person is competent to practice at an entry level standard.

Unfortunately, there are plenty of credentialed individuals out there that have never scanned a patent in their life! Sonography Canada wanted to avoid that and protect patients and therefore designed their credentialing system to try and combat this.

If possible, talk to as many people as you can. Speak to the teachers at the program, existing students, graduates and anyone else you feel can provide information on the program you are considering. They will provide a unique perspective that will allow you to make an informed decision about the program and the profession.

Prerequisites:

Most colleges or universities post their requirements for application. It is very important that you read these and know what is required for entry into the program. Some are completely high school based, but most require a few years of university or even a degree. Do you have what they want? This is a critical step in your decision as the school will not accept you unless these courses are complete. Are you willing to undertake the time and expense? If they are complete do you feel that your GPA is high enough to warrant consideration?

Essay:

Some if not most schools will ask you to fill out an essay or a series of essay questions regarding your interest in the program and background. These must be answered carefully so take your time! Look for some of the possible questions later in this chapter.

Volunteer Work:

Some if not all programs will require you to have some medical volunteer process and that will usually relate to ultrasound in some fashion. These will vary with each program. Some will require a day of job shadowing and some will require a week! Make sure you can check off that box.

This is a potentially difficult pre-requisite to accomplish so it is better to try and get this done as soon as you can. Departments are traditionally very busy and may not want to take the time away from patients to show you the way things are done. They may limit the number of job shadow requests to one a week or even one a month! Some are private and rely on numbers for profit, so you are slowing them down and costing them money! Some might say they do not want to allow you in due to privacy issues.

There are a multitude of reasons why departments might refuse you coming to observe. Do not be offended or get discouraged and try a different facility or lab as they all have different policies on job shadow requests. In the end it is usually in their best interest to allow you to observe because if you are successful, they will be the ones trying to actively recruit you!

Medical:

Some if not most schools will require you to complete a medical statement. It might be as simple as a questionnaire or they might want a complete physical. Some schools will require a criminal records check and even drug testing as a pre-requisite.

Application Steps:

It is fair to say that the application process is a long and tedious one. For summative purposes, the steps will usually include:

- You will be required to have in most cases the correct post-secondary pre-requisites in order before you apply. Count on there being a minimum grade level you will have to achieve.
- The college/university will require you to have all personal health documentation - like immunizations - up to date before they will accept your application. Ask for a list and then get them up to date well before hand.
- The application itself will include a multitude of questions. Some or all of them will be essay questions about yourself. How is your creative writing? Get someone to prufread it!
- There is an interview, and the panel is usually ruthless because in the end they want to have successful candidates in their program. Ultrasound is a unique training process, so the interview is tailored to look for suitable candidates. Practice questions in Appendix B.

- The number of applications to the number of spots can be as high as 10:1 or 15:1. How are you a better candidate than the rest of the crowd?
- There is usually a non-refundable application fee that must be paid when you apply. Sounds silly but I knew a very well qualified person that applied only to miss the deadline because she did not pay the fee and her application was rejected!

Application Questions:

There can be quite a variety of questions that are asked on the application. Most times it is an electronic document that you can type in and submit, but some facilities want you to print it out and then hand write. Thankfully when I went through, I could type mine in or I would not have been allowed in based on my terrible penmanship alone!

Some sample questions may include:

- What are the reasons you selected this program?
- Describe the reasons you believe that a career in imaging is a good fit for you.
- What are your personal strengths (describe the skills and aptitudes you feel would make you a successful candidate in this program)?
- What is your related experience?
- Academic or course work: Describe your post-secondary courses and provide supporting transcripts.
- You are applying for a program that usually has a significantly higher number of applicants than there are spaces. What do you feel sets you apart from the other applicants?

Bear in mind that a lot of these questions may be asked in the interview. Keep a copy of your application so when the interview time comes you do not give a different answer but expand on the one you wrote down!

Interviews:

People hate interviews. They get cold sweats thinking about being scrutinized and the pressure of the whole experience.

Some people love them!

Ok yes, it is because they not quite right in the head. But if you have made it to the interview there are a few simple steps you can do to ensure that you will be one of the candidates considered.

By far the most important thing you must do is prepare. Research everything possible about ultrasound then all you can about the current state of it in your area. After that, look for everything you can involving the training and then it is to your benefit to find someone that works in the field and ask them about applicable topics regarding the profession.

The second thing that is just as important as research is practice! It is not enough just to know about ultrasound and its topics, you must be able to converse about them in a coherent manner.

Grab a friend, parent or co-worker and get them to ask you some of the questions in appendix B. It will provide you some great feedback on where you can improve and the person "interviewing" you will notice areas you can improve.

Although most people loathe to do this, setting up a camera and videoing yourself answering the questions is a great thing to try.

One personal example I like to give from my interview was when researching all things ultrasound and the current state of it, there was something on the application that seemed a bit different. The program was not accepting applications from people outside my home province. At the time there was a critical shortage of sonographers in the part of the country I lived in and they wanted people they trained to stay. How would this be accomplished? Logically recruiting people only from the immediate area would have a higher chance of remaining here.

Unfortunately, where I live, the pay is not that competitive, the taxes are high, the weather is incompatible with survival in the winter and most of it is isolated! There were a multitude of great reasons to stay (sarcasm being inches thick).

At the time I did not know what I wanted to do with my career or if we wanted to stay in the area. My wife and I had little ties to this city and the salary/tax situation was more attractive elsewhere. Also, I wanted to go where I could utilize all the skills that were taught in the program not just a subset of them. Being selfish, I wanted a facility that did both general and echocardiography with good support for a green sonographer.

If these thoughts were mentioned to the interview panel, they probably would not have looked favorably on this. This series of "wants" I had was not in alignment at all with the current state of the "needs" in the area.

Inevitably the question was asked. "If you are successful and complete the program, what are your intentions after you graduate?" I replied "I would like to work in a department that would utilize all of the skills I learned in the program. I understand that an entry level sonographer is still learning, and I would need the proper mentorship to truly become competent and confident."

Was that a lie? No. Did I mention I would remain in the province after I graduated? No. Did I acknowledge the important fact that a green sonographer is still learning after finishing school? Yes, because it was an important point I discovered in my research.

The answer had an unexpected effect I learned several years later. All seven people on the interview panel thought "yes, my facility could do all that for him."

Even though it looked very casual and there was even a pause for a few seconds to make it look like I was thinking about my reply. The truth is I practiced and argued the response with my wife for week and a half before the interview took place because there was a good chance it was coming.

If you prepare well for an interview it is much like going into an exam and having all the answers. All you must do is *prepare* and *practice*.

Local issues that the panel might ask you will vary depending on current situations in your area, but I can give you a list some of the more common questions that interviewers might ask. See appendix B for some of the questions to practice

Interview Strategies:

A lot of times when it comes to ultrasound interviews, they are looking for people that will make good sonographers but also individuals that will survive the course! Do not be surprised in an interview that the panel will ask you what your greatest weakness is and then try to exploit it! When this occurs, try turning a negative into a positive. A note of caution, this might need a bit of - you guessed it - practice.

In my ultrasound interview they zeroed in on my lack of patient care because my initial certification was in pathology. Patients there (or pieces of them) tend not to talk back too much! They asked how I would deal with this lack of patient experience in a patient centric field. My response:

"Absolutely this is an area in which I am lacking and that is a major reason I have selected ultrasound as a field of study. I consider myself a 'people person' and my current career has a profound lack of patient interaction. I understand that ultrasound deals with patients in a unique way and a lot of time is spent with them during the scan. This is different from other imaging modalities and I consider my lack of patient contact to be an advantage because I am not unlearning a different method of patient care and then re-learning the most effective method. I have no preconceived bad habits and am ready to tackle a new skill properly and quickly!"

So that was a little thick but one thing I can do is talk with conviction especially when I have been coached. I can also talk a lot when it is the truth and is genuine. Be truthful and genuine!

Another aspect of exploiting a weakness might come in the form of questions that perhaps skirt close grey areas ethically. In the interest of selecting candidates that will survive the course the panel might start to inquire about aspects of your personal life. Do you have children? What are their ages? Why did you quit university? Colleges and universities usually do not do this, but some still do. Be aware that these types of questions might be something asked in your interview.

Regardless of questions asked the old and standard interview rules still apply.

- Show up 10-15 minutes early.
- Bring a copy of your resume.
- Dress appropriately.
- Be aware of your body language and smile.
- Have your questions ready to ask at the end of the interview.
- If possible - relax and have fun!

I did say "if possible" on the last one.

When the interview is completed, write down all the questions you can remember. I would suggest that you make notes on how you think you did or how you could improve.

Rejection.

Taking into consideration the ratio of applicants to positions, this is a very real possibility. You ask yourself "I have all the pre-requisites, my grades were good/excellent, I felt I did well on the application and interview so why was I not selected?"

Traditionally it is not a simple formula that the committee uses to say yea or nay.

It is very easy to say and very difficult to hear but do your best not to get discouraged! There are many sonographers I know that did not make it into training the first try. Most colleges acknowledge that you are tenacious and will accept that you are serious if you re-apply.

Before you fire up the application process again, there are some things you should review.

Self-Evaluation

It is time to be brutally honest with yourself and this is hard to do. Re-read the application you submitted (remember you saved a copy!) and look at it again but from the perspective of a person that has been through the process now. Are there any things that come across as insincere or poorly written? Was there questions the interview panel emphasized that you did not cover or did not think were important in the application?

It is time to get your red pen out and start revising. After all you are much better informed with respect to the wants and needs of the training and school.

Look at your notes from the interview. Were there any specific questions that you did not answer as well as you would have liked? Were there ones that caught you off guard? This is the time you must objectively look at how the interview went. As mentioned previously it is very hard to admit you were weak and not up to the level they required. As hard a lesson this is, it is a great way in which we can build on and improve.

How were your required grades with the pre-requisites? This might be the hardest and most time-consuming aspect of self-reflection as it has the potential for being the most difficult thing to rectify. Re-taking courses is hard and an expensive thing to do. On the flip side if you think this is an area where you believe you did not shine and decide to fix it, the selection committee would acknowledge the effort and take this in to account if they had to decide on you candidacy again. Trust me, if they did not know you went to all the effort, I would casually let slip in the interview that this was done.

Get some feedback from the experts. OK, so they turned you down… Jerks! Buggers! Hit something (soft) and take a few deep breaths. Now it is time to get back to work. Contact the program head (via phone if possible) and thank them for their time and consideration. Tell them you respect their decision for not allowing you to enter the program but would like some feedback on what areas were lacking on your part. I have been turned down for jobs on several occasions and I have always contacted the lead interviewer and asked this. It is a fair question, and they should give you a sincere answer. Be ready to write down what they say and start to act on their observations.

Rejection sucks! You have so much belief in yourself and know you can be successful in the training or job and it is a crushing blow when you get turned down. Believe me, pick yourself up, brush yourself off and move on to the next step. If you are passionate about wanting this as a career, then keep working at it.

People supposedly say, "when a door closes a window opens." I disagree. I say "When the door closes… I kick open the door!" Take control and kick that door back open.

Part III - Training

After you have applied and interviewed you got into the program! Congratulations! Buckle up!
After taking university, a college diploma and multiple certification programs I thought I would
breeze this course. It helped being prepared for certain aspects of ultrasound training, but this
was nothing like I encountered before!

Training in Ultrasound:

The ultrasound training is a unique process. It involves a great deal of book learning that in-
cludes physics, relational anatomy/physiology and patient care. Then there is also the scanning
(clinical) portion of the course. The thing that makes ultrasound a unique course is that it is a
subjective learning process. This means that it is incredibly hard to teach and equally difficult to
learn as the subject matter you are scanning, and the scanning process are constantly chang-
ing. It will require an enormous amount of time and dedication!

The training, like any other training program, can be a very fun process depending on your fellow students. Usually when you are learning normal anatomy the scanning you do is on each
other, so you literally get to know your co-workers inside and out! Many sonographers have
said it is this type of learning process that made the course very enjoyable.

Work Environment:

As with anything in health care that involves working with patients, there are a great deal of positive and rewarding points in addition to certain unpleasant aspects you must deal with.

The ability to help and care for people is one of the greatest reasons for people entering the
field. It is incredibly satisfying to be presented with an ill patient and a clinical question the doc-
tors cannot answer and be able to send them away with the information that will help the clinical
team provide appropriate treatment.

There are of course some negative aspects to the environment. Patients can be rude, demand-
ing and even physically abusive! Thankfully, this is rare, so the grateful, polite and humorous
ones far outweigh the former. Another thing to consider is that the qualities making a great sonographer can often make for difficult co-workers. This is primarily the exception rather than the
rule but there have been some extremely loud disagreements and explosive conversations in
ultrasound departments!

Put several anal-retentive, type-A control freaks in the same department for an extended period
and it is just a matter of time before the fireworks present themselves!

<u>**Ultrasound Training Courses**</u>

As mentioned in the past ultrasound training is a unique process. But what will you be expected to learn in the training program? Here is a sample of the types of courses you will be required to take and pass. Some universities and colleges will have additional ones, but these are the main ones.

<u>**Physics:**</u>

This is usually a word that strikes fear in the heart of normal people. As with interviews, I consider myself extremely abnormal!

Whether you like it or hate it this is the course that must be passed so you have a better understanding of how to manipulate sound waves to produce diagnostic images. The good thing about physics as it relates to ultrasound is that it is very basic compared to university courses that can be more theoretical in nature.

With a little work and a decent teacher, self-proclaimed math morons do very well in this subject.

Some of the areas you will cover are:

Sound wave characteristics
Artifacts
Ultrasound hardware
Safety and bio effects

<u>**Abdominal Ultrasound:**</u>

This course will encompass sonography of all the abdominal organs. You will learn about the pancreas, liver, kidneys, gallbladder, biliary system, spleen and abdominal vasculature. The course will cover not only anatomy/physiology but relational anatomy and pathology (where one organ is in relation to another spatially). There will be a scanning portion as well that will be at least half if not more of the total time.

<u>**Obstetrics and Gynecology:**</u>

This is the course that initially draws a great many candidates to the program as it is the most widely known aspect of ultrasound. It is also one of the toughest and longest courses and the one people usually have the most trouble with apart from physics.

Obstetrics covers all things baby and gynecology covers all things "lady!"

<u>**Obstetrics:**</u>

This is the area that undoubtedly gets the most press and labels ultrasound as a "fun" profession.

All fun aside there are serious objectives in obstetrical ultrasound scanning the general public does not usually appreciate. Obstetrics covers all thing babies from early pregnancy to late fetal assessments you are scanning to make sure that mom and baby are doing ok.

A lot of the scans are just like the ones you see on television or perhaps experienced yourself. Sonographers scan looking for all the normal anatomy and provide a report of their findings with the projected due date from the measurements.

It can be one of the most stressful areas to work on mentally and physically. Physically you are spending most of your scan time in very ergonomically unfriendly positions. It can be difficult mentally as you will find fetal abnormalities or even fetal death in your career not to mention your spatial reasoning is taxed trying to scan a moving target!

Gynecology:

This is an area that is obviously dealing with female health issues other than pregnancy.

Gynecology ultrasound involves scanning the uterus, ovaries and all the associated structures involving female anatomy.

There are some particularly tricky situations that are specific in dealing in this area.

- The uterus and ovaries are usually located posterior (behind) the bowel in the lower abdomen. Ultrasound cannot penetrate gas so anything posterior to bowel is "gassed out" and we cannot visualize it. To counteract this, we fill the patient's bladder to provide a medium ultrasound can penetrate easily (fluid) and at the same time it pushes the bowel up in the abdomen and out of the way. The bad and "tricky" part is that the patient requires a full bladder! Then you put cold gel on them and start to push. It unfortunately is the physics of ultrasound and not just us being mean!

- Another test that usually goes with the abdominal scan mentioned above is the internal or endovaginal scan. This involves inserting an elongated probe about 4-6 inches into the vagina and doing the same protocol scan as mentioned above. the reason this is done is that the transducer used is a higher frequency (and resolution) that allows you to get closer and investigate the organs more effectively. The bad part is that this is obviously an *internal* exam and is very intrusive. This can be very uncomfortable for the patient when dealing with male sonographers and I have had patients insist that the exam be performed by a female. I respect the fact that people are not willing to allow me to perform the exam irrespective of the reasons.

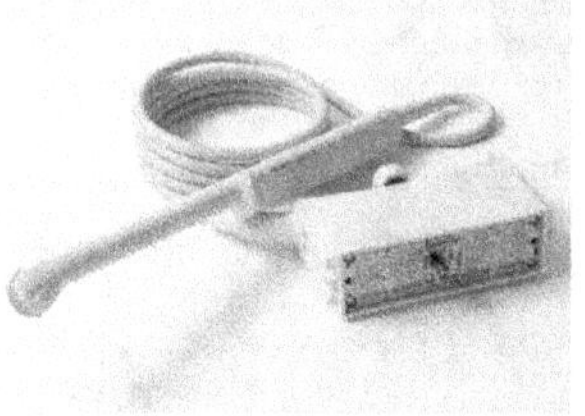

Small Parts:

This is the area that deals with what are affectionally called small and squishy bits. The thyroid gland, testicles, salivary glands and superficial masses (lumps and bumps) fit into this category. These are scans that are looking for abnormalities using high resolution linear or flat probes.

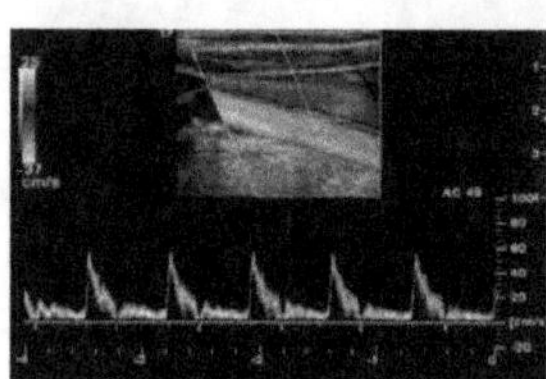

Vascular:

This is sometimes an included course of study or it can be a separate certification altogether. Vascular include all things dealing with blood vessels and their components. Most of the time carotid ultrasound to exclude a stenosis, abdominal aorta or a DVT (arm or leg) study are usually included as part of a general ultrasound program. But advanced testing like shunts, portal hypertension and renal artery Doppler studies might be limited to a vascular specialist.

Cardiac:

Cardiac ultrasound is a specialty area of ultrasound that involves scanning the heart. Some ultrasound programs include cardiac training, but a good number are dedicated just to cardiac scanning. This area teaches you to scan the heart and gather/interpret all the 2 dimensional and Doppler information the protocol requires. There is a large volume of information and It is challenging to learn!   Once you are done, expect it to take months if not years to get comfortable and confident in your scanning.

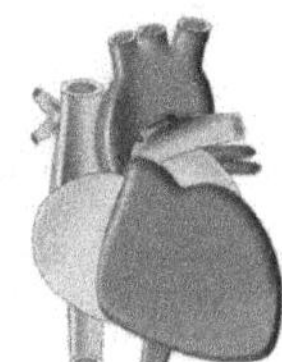

MSK

Musculoskeletal scanning can be included to some degree in most courses but usually is picked up after you graduate and have some experience from one of the general courses. This will teach you how to scan and interpret injuries and abnormalities involving muscles and tendons of shoulders, knees and extremities (hands, wrists, feet, etc.).

Ophthalmic:

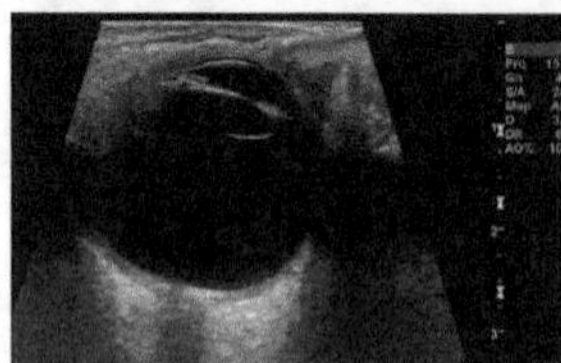

This type of ultrasound is not usually taught in general ultrasound training and is acquired as a specialty certificate after graduation. It involves scanning the eye for potential pathologies like retinal detachment, lens dislocation or possible tumors.

Breast:

This is a specialty area as well. Sometimes it is included with a general ultrasound training course or can be taught later as an additional course.

Scanning Components:

A significant amount of scanning will be required with all the courses. It makes sense as this is what a sonographer does!

Both didactic and scanning portions are equally important as one teaches you the theoretical knowledge of why we look for things and how they are relevant in the clinical setting. The scanning portion will teach you the physical scanning to locate, identify and document any abdominal organ or pathological process. There are usually many very intelligent people breeze the didactic portion only to have trouble or not pass the scan lab.   You MUST be able to pass both!

Luckily, programs are set up for this and handle any issues or problems people might have with this type of subjective learning. In clinical you will be presented with many diverse cases so you will graduate with the skills to be a competent entry level sonographer. As with any new skill or job learning is ongoing and you will get better with experience. Courses focus on giving you the baseline and making you competent to practice.

When you are in the non-clinical portion of your school (at the college) your scanning might be limited to volunteers or your fellow classmates. When you move into the clinical stage of your education if will focus almost entirely on development of your scanning skills.

Other courses you might encounter in training could include:

Patient Care:

There is usually a course on basic patient care as this is a health care field and learning how to handle patients is an important thing to be familiar with. Do you know how to transfer a patient that is very unsteady? Do you know how to hook up oxygen and control the proper flow rate? Can you set up a sterile area for the radiologist to do a pleural tap? No? Well this is the course that will give you that background.
If you are coming in from an allied health field that has a strong patient care background, ask if you can challenge or transfer credit from a similar course you may already have taken. This might save you some tuition and more importantly allow you to spend more time on the other heavy courses you are in.

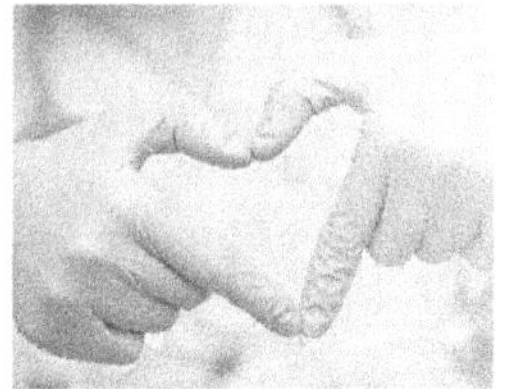

Medical Terminology:

This is a course required in the program or may have to be completed before you enter the program. It will give you the fundamentals of speaking in the medical language - and it can be quite the language sometimes! Do you know what an anastomosis is? Neither does the spell checker on my word processor but this course will help!

Interprofessional Relations:

Inter-professional relations a course that is present in some programs and there is debate on 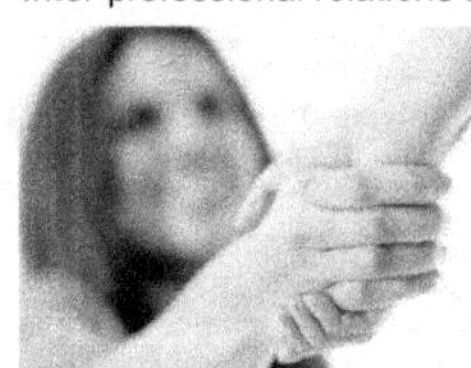 how useful it is. As the name of the course indicates it will introduce you to other members of the medical profession and how they relate to what you do in ultrasound. In the day to day work environment ultrasound and cardiology work as a part of a huge team. It is good to know what role we play and how we integrate into health care.

As with the patient care course, if you come from a medical background you may be able to challenge or get an exemption from it.

Repetitive Strain Injuries (RSI):

One of the things people who work and teach in the field ask potential candidates is if they have researched any information regarding repetitive strain injury. The answers I have received ranged from slight concern and indifference to someone (actually) rolling their eyes at me! I do not push it... No pun intended!

Unfortunately, it is a fact that a significant amount of people that perform ultrasound do not last till retirement. A lot of the people working in ultrasound that do make it to retirement have  moved into management, teaching or applications due to injuries sustained while scanning.

Once while doing a lecture explaining ultrasound to a laboratory group, I asked for a volunteer and gave them a three-pound weight. Then they were instructed to put their arm straight out and bend their elbow, so the hand was pointing to the floor. Holding the weight in that hand they were instructed them lean over slightly sideways towards the outstretched arm and hold that position for the entire presentation. About 15 minutes into the presentation they were asked how they were doing. As they stretched and moved around getting some feeling back into their arms and torso, they were told they just had the equivalent of stress that one echo puts on your body!

Now you have eight more to do today!

Pain in your hands, arms, shoulder, back and neck are your new reality. Massage therapy is going to be a must and a gym membership (that you use) is a very good idea. Some things might exacerbate the problem like doing all the same exam (echo or obstetrics) but make no mistake about it pain is going to be present in your career.

The chances and intensity can be reduced if you do several things. As mentioned previously, stretching between patients, mixing up the type of scan you do and engaging in some sort of physical activity outside of work would all be beneficial. Other things you want to research or incorporate include:

- Micro breaks in your scanning. These are small periods of rest when you are not actively scanning. When doing measurements or freezing an image you do not need to maintain pressure on the patient. Take that 10-15 seconds and rest your arm. This is difficult to do while learning but gets easier as you gain experience.
- Set up your patient properly. Instructors will emphasize during your training program that having the patient close to you and using your body weight rather than arm/shoulder strength will enhance your image quality and reduce potential injury.
- Set up your equipment properly. Ultrasound units and stretchers are designed so they can be articulated in an infinite number of ways to accommodate all body sizes. Use this functionality to position you and your patient in the most comfortable position possible.
- Consult with occupational therapy or a kinesiologist. These are the experts in body mechanics and can help guide you in proper set up of your work environment and proper body mechanics. Physiotherapists are great, but their primary focus usually is rehabilitation after an injury. Try to prevent it in the first place!
- Types and numbers of patients. Obviously, the more patients you do the stress on your body is increased and the rest between patients is decreased. Types refer to inpatient versus outpatient scans. People that are in the hospital tend to be less able to transfer themselves and require assistance to move. There have been many injuries in my workplace involving sonographers that have tried to prevent patients from falling or using bad transferring techniques. Get proper training and help when moving people.
- Listen to your body! If it is uncomfortable to do something or painful stop it and find a different technique!

If you are asked about knowing anything regarding injuries in ultrasound, I would suggest telling them you understand how they happen and are researching strategies to prevent them.

The Sonographers Role:

The sonographer's primary role is to scan and interpret the area of interest to provide a technical impression of what is observed. The best and most concise job description is reiterated by a very experienced sonologist I had the pleasure of working with. He said, "answer the question, that's your job!"

Sonographers perform this function under the direction of an interpreting clinician (usually a radiologist or cardiologist). They will make a diagnosis based on the clinical information and images you provide then consult with the referring physician regarding clinical treatment of the patient.

There is an important distinction between the roles of the sonographer and interpreting clinician. Sonographers are focused on the *technical* aspects of scanning and providing the answer to the clinical question whereas the clinician focuses on the provided images and manages the patient *clinically.*

Patients often ask us for results and unfortunately it is not in our scope of practice to provide them. This constitutes a very grey area in different locations and some sonographers feel more comfortable than others sharing information. Realistically it is our job to provide the clinicians with the ultrasound information and the clinician combines this with all the other relevant patient data then counsels the patient.

This is only the sonographer's primary role. Other aspects sonographers get involved with include:
- Equipment evaluation and selection.
- Development of new protocols and research.
- Clinical and didactic instruction of sonography students.
- Quality control of staff and/or equipment.
- Guidance during interventional procedures (biopsies).
- Sales and application training for ultrasound equipment.
- Informatics (RIS/PACS) duties.
- Maintenance and cleaning of equipment.

<u>**What Exactly is Ultrasound?**</u>

Ultrasound is sound that has a frequency in excess of 20,000 Hz (Hertz) or 20 KHz (Kilohertz). This frequency is too high for humans to hear.

The ultrasound used in medical imaging is significantly higher than that. It usually ranges in the 2 – 20 MHz (Megahertz) or 20,000,000 Hz!

Ultrasound is introduced into the body by a probe called a transducer. Inside the transducer are special crystals that vibrate at these high frequencies in short bursts. In between these short bursts they "listen" for the sound that bounces back from inside the body. Based on the time it takes for the sound to get back to the probe and the intensity of the signal, the machine makes up the image from this data.

Since ultrasound is made up of sound there is no ionizing radiation as in other forms of medical imaging. This makes it ideal for investigating sensitive tissues like in obstetrics. It is important to note that ultrasound is a form of energy that is introduced into the body and there are potential heat and mechanical side effects from it. Even though these potential bio-effects are low, they are still present. Sonographers are trained to recognize and reduce the potential hazards of ultrasound energy in the body.

It is important to note that ultrasound waves rely on a path that has the same relative density to propagate. If it encounters a large density mismatch (bone or air) the sound wave will be absorbed or reflected, and image data cannot be collected deep to this. That is why ultrasound is not the best modality for investigating bone, bowel (gas) or lungs.

Appendix A

Glossary:

AAA: Abdominal aortic aneurysm. A dilation of the abdominal aorta that when left
                untreated may progress to rupture.

Anal Retentive: Being obsessive about attention to detail.

ARDMS: American Registry of Diagnostic Medical Sonographers. This is a U.S.
                based licensing body.
Anastomosis: a connection or opening between two things (especially cavities or passages)
                that are normally diverging or branching.

Clinical: Relating to the observation and treatment of actual patients rather than theoretic-
                cal or laboratory study.

Clinical Instructor: A person that instructs in a clinical (scanning) environment.

DVT: Deep vein thrombosis or clot in a deep venous system.

MFM: Maternal Fetal Medicine.

MSK: Musculoskeletal. A type of ultrasound to help diagnose sprains, strains and tears
                in muscles and tendons.

RDCS: Registered Diagnostic Cardiac Sonographer. The ADRMS credential for cardiac
                sonographers. To attain this certification, you must pass the SPI (physics)
                examination and one of the pediatric or adult cardiac examinations.

RDMS: Registered Diagnostic Medical Sonographer. The ARDMS credential for
                generalist sonographers. To attain this, you must pass the SPI (physics)
                examination and one of the generalist examinations.

RSI: Repetitive strain injury. A type of injury people that do repetitive tasks are prone.

RVT: Registered Vascular Technologist. The ARDMS credential for vascular
                sonographers.

Shunt: A hole that allows fluid to travel from one area to another.

SC: Sonography Canada the Canadian licensing body for ultrasound.

Sonographer: A sonographer is a healthcare professional who specializes in the use of ultra-
                sonic imaging devices to produce diagnostic images.

Sonologist: A doctor, usually a radiologist, that specializes in the interpretation of ultrasound
                images.

SPI: Sonography Principles and Instrumentation exam. This is the old ARDMS
                "physics" examination.

Stenosis: A tightening or narrowing.

Technical: Having specialized knowledge usually involving a mechanical or scientific field.

Technician: Not a sonographer…

Transducer: The ultrasound "probe." It converts electrical signals to physical vibrations and
                vice-versa.

Appendix B: Sample Ultrasound Interview Questions:

Not to flog an obvious point to death but it is extremely important that you practice these! The ones in bold are question that are most likely encountered in sonography interviews.   These have been compiled from multiple sources and from questions I have asked candidates myself!

Warm up Questions

Who are you?

Tell me about yourself? This is a very common interview question so be ready for it! Try to sum up who you are and what led you to be interested in applying for ultrasound. Oh, yeah and try to do it in 30-45 seconds!

General Questions

• Who is your hero and why?
• What were your favorite and least favorite courses in college?
• Of all the people, dead or alive, who would you most like to have dinner with and why?
• What are you passionate about?
• How can you tell if someone is compassionate?
• What negative experiences from your background made it clear that you wanted to pursue healthcare?
• **Why should we accept you into the program? What sets you apart?** This is a very important question, be prepared for some variation of it!
• **Is there anything that you want us to know about you that we have not asked you?** This is another common interview question they will probably ask. This is where you need to sneak in some positive comments about yourself. Try not to brag too much!

Self- Assessment

• What kind of thing do you feel most confident in doing?
• **Can you describe for me a difficult obstacle you have had to overcome? How did you handle it?**
• How do you feel this experience affected your personality or ability?

- **Describe your greatest strengths and weakness.**
- **What do you think are the most importance characteristics and abilities a person must possess to become a successful sonographer? How do you rate yourself in these areas? See section 1 for some of the possibilities.**   Expect this one.
- Do you consider yourself a self-starter? If so, explain why and give examples.
- What do you consider to be your greatest achievements to date? Why?
- What things give you the greatest satisfaction in school and in your life?

Personal

- **How did you prepare for this interview?** This is a question that is common in the facility I am currently employed in. It is a great question that totally threw me the first time I encountered it. Telling about how you got interested in ultrasound, your research into it as a career and your prep leading up to the interview are things you should mention.
- Describe yourself in three words.
- How would you describe yourself as a person?
- How would your friends describe you?
- If I were to ask your academic advisor about your ability as a candidate for this program, what would he/she say?
- **What leadership positions have you had?**
- Tell me specifically what you did in the civic activities in which you participate (leading, sports, current events, etc.).
- **What do you do in your spare time?**
- In what kind of activities have you been involved?
- What are your hobbies?
- What was the last book you read?
- What makes you laugh and why?
- Which qualities would you want to pass down to your children?
- What about yourself would you change if you could?
- What three material objects are most important to you?

Education

- **What special aspects of your education or training have prepared you for admission into this program?**
- What courses would you recommend to futures applicants?
- Do you think that your grades are a good index of your abilities?
- What was your toughest subject in college?

Stress

- What causes you the most stress in your life?
- What things frustrate you the most? How do you usually cope with them?
- **Sonography school is a high-pressure situation, how do you normally handle stress and what do you normally do to relieve stress?**
- What would you do if a Radiologist or an ER physician screamed at you?
- What would you do if a physician, sonographer, or professor humiliated you in front of others?
- What has been the highest-pressure situation you have been under in recent years? How did you cope with it?
- When you need counseling for a personal problem, who do you talk to?
- **What is your typical way of dealing with conflict? Give me an example.**

• **Tell me about a time when you were able to successfully deal with another person even when that individual may not have personally liked you (or vice versa).**

Qualifications & Experience

• What work experience have you had?
• What health care experience have you had?
• How have you contributed to your community?
• **Do you like to work alone or with other people?**
• **Are you able to function independently without supervision?**
• Do you use a prioritization scheme to complete tasks?

Team and Teamwork Questions

• **Have you ever worked as part of a team?**
• **Give an example of a time that you contributed to a group effort.**
• Do you feel you work more effectively on a one on one basis or in a group setting?
• **If you were the team leader and there was a conflict between team members, how would you attempt to resolve the conflict?**

Creativity

• In your experience, what have you done that you consider truly creative?
• Can you think of a problem that you have encountered when the old solutions did not work and when you came up with a new solution?
• Of your creative accomplishments big or small, at work or home, what gave you the most satisfaction? What kind of problems have people recently called upon you to solve? Tell me what you have devised.

Decisiveness

• **Do you consider yourself to be a thoughtful, analytical or do you usually make up your mind fast? Give an example.**
• What was your most difficulty decision in the last 6 months? What made it difficult?
• The last time you did not know what decision to make, what did you do?
• How do you go about making an important decision affecting your career?
• **What was the last major problem you confronted? What action did you take on it?**

Leadership

• **Have you held a leadership position in an organization?**
• What approach do you take in getting your people to accept your ideas or goals?
• What specifically do you do to set an example for coworkers?
• What sort of leader do your people feel you are? Are you satisfied?
• How would you describe your basic leadership style? Give specific examples of how you practice this?

Sonography Specific Questions

- **Why do you want to be a sonographer?**
- **If you want to help people, why not social work or nursing?**
- Explain your interest in the medical field, start at the beginning and be specific.
- What major influences in your life led you to your decision to pursue a career in sonography.
- What will you contribute to the profession?
- **What qualities do you look for in a healthcare worker?**
- You have very little experience in the medical setting, therefore, how do you know you want to get your hands dirty and become part of the medical world?
- What experiences have you had in the community that demonstrate a commitment to the medical field?
- **What scare you the most about the DMS program?**
- **What makes you think that you will be successful in the DMS program?**
- Why study DMS when you have so many talents?
- **Do you know what a real sonographer's life is like?**
- **What do you need to work on to be a good sonographer?**
- What is the one thing that would prevent you from going through a sonography program and completing your education?
- What are your standards for judging success?
- **What will you do if you do not get into the program this year?**
- What would you say is the most important medical development to date?
- What do you think will be the biggest challenge in healthcare in the next 10 years?
- What would you do to remedy health care issues in the US?
- Who do you think about credentialing and medical reimbursement?

Ethical Issues

- Have you ever cheated on an exam?
- What would you do if you caught a close friend cheating in a course that you were also enrolled?
- Would you prefer to provide average care and help more patients, or would you prefer to provide excellent care and help fewer patients?

Other Questions

- Describe a situation in which you were able to use persuasion to successfully convince someone to see things your way.
- Describe a time when you were faced with a stressful situation in which you demonstrated your coping skills.
- Give me an example of a time when you used good judgment and logic in solving a problem.
- Give me an example of a time when you set a goal and were able to meet or achieve it.
- Give me a specific example of a time when you had to conform to a policy in which you did not agree.
- Tell me about a time when you had to go above and beyond the call of duty in order to get a job done.
- Give me an example of a time you had to make a split decision
- Tell me about a difficult decision that you had to make in the last year.
- Give me an example of a time when you tried to accomplish something and failed.
- **Give me an example of when you showed initiative and took the lead.**
- **Tell me about a recent situation in which you had to deal with a very upset customer or coworker.**

- Give me an example of a time when you motivated others.
- Give me an example of the time when you used your fact-finding skills to solve a problem.
- Describe a time when you anticipated potential problems and developed preventive measures.
- Tell me about a time when you were forced to make an unpopular decision.
- Describe a time when you set your sights too high (or too low).
- Tell me about a time when you missed an obvious solution to a problem.
- With your lack of experience, how do you expect to perform well in this program?
- **How would you handle a situation when a patient's religious of personal beliefs do not coincide with yours?**
- Sonographers are often in situations where they know the outcome of their patient's fate before anyone else. What will your coping mechanism be, when you are discussing an upcoming trip with a patient and you KNOW they will not be alive to take that trip?
- What strategies will you use to comfort a patient when she learns that her baby has a life-threatening diagnosis and will not survive birth?

Multiple Mini Interview:

Multiple mini interviews are becoming the new normal for selecting candidates in many of the medical professions. It consists of multiple stations each comprising a "mini interview" or individual scenario. They are designed to measure competencies like oral communication, social and non-verbal skills.

Since the potential students interact with multiple interviewers in several assessments it theoretically produces a more reliable measurement and limits interview biases by any single interviewer.

The set up for this format consists of six to ten stations and will take upwards of two hours. There is usually a two-minute prep period and then five to eight minutes of conversation about the presented topic.

To say the topics are wide ranging is again an understatement. Usually they are focused on each school's end goal of becoming a competent and working sonographer. Since you cannot prepare for the topics in advance be prepared to show them who you are and articulate why you are the best candidate. Showcase those interpersonal and critical thinking skills!

Possible interview stations may include:

- Scenarios involving interactions with an actor or a medical school's standardized patient.

- An essay writing station: this station may take longer than the others.

- A standard interview station.

- A teamwork station where candidates must work together to complete a task.

- An ethical scenario involving questions about social and policy implications.

- A "rest" station to help students catch their breath and relax.

An excellent online resource is available at: https://multipleminiinterview.com/

www.ingramcontent.com/pod-product-compliance
Lightning Source LLC
Chambersburg PA
CBHW071505150726
48000CB00006B/2703